Back Home – Simply Country

by
Judy Condon

Library of Congress Cataloging-in-Publications Data
Back Home – Simply Country by Judy Condon
ISBN 978-0-9843332-9-5

Oceanic Graphic Printing, Inc.
105 Main Street
Hackensack, NJ 07601

Printed in China

Layout and Design by Pat Lucas
Edited by Trent Michaels

Table of Contents

Introduction 5

Chapter 1 6
Audrey and Rich Rupert

Chapter 2 19
Barbara and Michael Burnett

Chapter 3 43
Eileen and Peter Litwin

Chapter 4 59
Maria and Rickey Walker

Chapter 5 70
Sandy and Gordon Mariner

Chapter 6 77
Carol and George Meekins

Chapter 7 92
Carolyn Carter

Chapter 8 106
Vera and Fran McCarthy

Chapter 9 118
Judy and Jeff Condon

About the Author

Judy Condon is a native New Englander, which is evident in her decorating style and the type of antiques she collects and sells. Her real passion is 19thC authentic dry red or blue painted pieces. While Judy enjoyed a professional career as a teacher, Principal, and Superintendent of Schools in Connecticut, Judy's weekends were spent at her antique shop, *Marsh Homestead Country Antiques*, located in Litchfield, Connecticut.

When her husband, Jeff, was relocated to Virginia, Judy accepted an early retirement from education and concentrated her energy and passion for antiques into a fulltime business. Judy maintains a website, *www.marshhomesteadantiques.com* and has been a Power Seller on eBay® for over 13 years under the name "superct".

Judy and her husband Jeff recently returned to their roots in New England and have completed renovating a 19thC cape in Massachusetts. Judy has five children and five grandchildren and enjoys reading, golf, bridge, tennis, and volunteering in the educational system in St Maarten. Judy does her best to provide teaching materials and children's books to the schools in St. Maarten with the hope of helping establish classroom libraries.

Judy's first 17 books in the "simply country" series, *Country on a Shoestring, Of Hearth and Home – Simply Country, A Simpler Time, Country Decorating for All Seasons, As Time Goes By, Country at Heart, Welcome Home – Simply Country, Home Again – Simply Country, The Warmth of Home, The Country Home, Simple Greens – Simply Country, The Country Life, Simply Country Gardens, The Spirit of Country, The Joy of Country, Holidays at a Country Home,* and *A Touch of Country* have been instant hits and most are in their second printing. Judy may be reached through her Website *www.marshhomesteadantiques.com*, by email at *marshhomestead@comcast.net*, or by phone at 877-381-6682.

Introduction

Two years ago, while photographing homes for one of my books, I was traveling through Massachusetts with a friend on our way to the next home. We were taking a "short cut" down a wooded country road, when we approached a small rise and I slammed on my brakes. Fortunately my friend was wearing a seat belt or I fear I might have propelled her through the windshield. I put the car in reverse and backed up to gaze longingly at a 19thC white Cape with a huge maple tree in front; woods and meadows surrounded by old stone walls. I sat for the longest time and knew right then, that was the house I had to live in one day. That was where I belonged. To my good fortune, a for sale sign gave the realtor's information and as I snapped pictures with my camera, my friend wrote down the information.

Jeff and I had planned on traveling and using our small RV when he retired in a few years so I had begun to sell our antiques in preparation to downsize. We had planned to store what was left for three or four years and see if we wanted to purchase another home at that time.

Each morning for eighteen months after that trip in New England, I looked online to see if the listing was still available; holding my breath that it had not been sold. The property

was listed with many additional acres which neither Jeff nor I had any interest in owning or paying taxes on. The price with the land made it out of our reach. As the months passed, I was having a more difficult time parting with our antiques, each of which, as you know, has a story with it and personal experience. My husband and I discussed our options at length and he, recognizing how important this was to me, revised our original plans to include a small house in New England for his retirement years. With a slow real estate market, we placed our Virginia home on the market anticipating a year or more to sell it. Within six weeks we had an offer with a contingency dependent upon our buyers selling their home. Three months went by and although Jeff had not even seen my "dream house" he trusted my judgment and encouraged me to go see it and later make an offer. Talk about the sign in the shops that says "your husband called and said you can buy whatever you want"!

In addition to a chapter on our 19thC New England cape and the renovations to it, *Back Home – Simply Country* includes the Delaware home of a man and his wife who occasionally has to turn down his offer to take her antiquing, the home of George and Carol Meekins, owners of *Country Treasures* in Maryland, a Connecticut home with a variety of unique eclectic collections, an Ohio home with wonderful painted pieces, a home in Indiana with his and her log home outbuildings, the home of a western Pennsylvania shop owner, and two homes where antique and contemporary pieces have been integrated beautifully; one home in Delaware and the other in Massachusetts.

Chapter 1

Audrey and Rich Rupert

Audrey and Rich Rupert have known each other since high school in Monongahela Valley, Pennsylvania, and have been married 48 years. Both are collectors that gravitate toward what was called "Early American" in the 1970's. They started attending auctions and began to accumulate enough antiques that Rich constructed a building to house it all. Then a neighbor inquired about renting space and a dealer asked the same thing and soon Rich was in business renting to 10 dealers in his large building. That was in 1988. His business is called *Rustique Antiques*. Around that same time, Audrey was beginning to formulate a plan of her own. Audrey would often visit a nearby primitive shop and one day was taken upstairs to see the shop owner's home. From that point on, Audrey knew she wanted her home to look the same. She got a job at a local hospital and convinced Rich that they needed an addition to their 1972 home. Audrey decided to gradually redecorate every room in her newly discovered style.

An old farm cart in early red wash sits under the large maple.

Further up the driveway, an early wheelbarrow holding potted plants stands beside a vintage farm tool.

The barrel in the side yard hides an old pump and provides a pedestal for a pot of gorgeous flowers.

Walking into the addition at the front of the house, a visitor steps into a large room with not one but two early farm tables and magnificent early cupboards filled with collections and treasures.

The table in red wash dates to the 18thC and has a stretcher base-note its unique five drawers.

The butler's tray was a gift from Rich to Audrey; it holds a pewter tea set and early stoneware pitcher.

The cupboard in black was made by a furniture restorer friend from old boards. Audrey displays an old birdcage on top. Amidst the pewter and yellowware bowls on the shelves, Audrey displays select pieces of Bennington Tavernware.

The large corner cupboard was found with thick white paint; Rich and Audrey cautiously removed it to expose the natural wood stain. The early child's wagon below is filled with bears and pumpkins.

Audrey found the old rope couch at Spring hill Furniture in Greensburg, Pennsylvania, where she buys many of her country accessories.

The walnut corner cupboard is filled with yellowware pieces including two rolling pins on the bottom shelf. Bittersweet vines and a black crow spruce up the top.

The bucket bench with apron is filled with more of Audrey's brown-banded yellowware bowls.

The second farm table in the room dates to the 1800's and features a cherry base; it came from a monastery.

The large dough bowl with mustard paint in the center of the table is one of Audrey's favorite pieces; she particularly likes the early string repair. Pieces of fruit nestle with pot pouri.

Stacking two long benches provides Audrey with additional display space for her stoneware. On the bottom bench, she has stacked three early seed boxes.

Audrey and Rich were drawn to another long bench not only because of the remnants of early green paint but because of its narrow seat. The doll in the center was made by James Cramer and is one of Audrey's favorites.

The spectacular 19thC dry sink with dry bittersweet paint, probably original to Virginia, was purchased at a Sandi Hart auction in Pennsylvania. Audrey said it was the ONE antique they bought that year at a time when they couldn't afford it. However, they've had no regrets.

Audrey and Rich purchased the unique Shaker butter churn in blue/gray paint after it was deaccessioned from the Shaker Heights Museum.

Two bail-handled pantry boxes in paint are stacked on top of the New England hanging cupboard with just enough blue paint. Audrey displays a few of her Barbara Stein animals; she is only missing three in her collection.

Rich and Audrey's daughter-in-law meticulously measured the floor and painted the faux border and oak leaves to resemble a stenciled floor cloth!

Many baskets hang from the beams in the living room of the original house. Audrey married a hanging glass front cupboard and table in the corner; the cupboard holds a collection of small redware houses. A Barbara Stein camel stands on top beside an early basket.

A massive stone fireplace with raised hearth fills nearly the entire wall on the opposite side of the room. A collection of standing candlemold surrounds a Barbara Stein elephant. Two foot warmers can be seen on the hearth.

Audrey uses an old doll's sleigh to hold two potted plants on an end table. The tin candleholder was purchased at The Strawberry Crow in Ligonier, Pennsylvania. A jelly cupboard at the far end of the room stands beneath a large shelf displaying stoneware, a folk art house, and more stuffed folk art animals.

A garland of crab apples is strung across the front.

The table in the middle of the kitchen is old and has been refinished. The old stove was purchased at The Strawberry Crow. Barely visible is a Barbara Stein owl peeking out from behind the lamp on top of the early pie safe with attic surface. The apothecary on top came from an old department store in Morgantown, West Virginia.

Audrey filled the old jelly cupboard with red wash and bead board doors with her cocoa tin collection. Stacks of pantry boxes and buckets stand on top.

Rich and Audrey painted their cupboards black to give the room a more aged look. I had never photographed a kitchen with black cabinets and I must say it was striking; the bricks behind the counters really stood out.

Old tin lidded jars of varying sizes and lids hold a variety of drieds. A cutter rests beside two sugar cones.

A large collection of tins from local grocer Clover Farms are displayed over the stove. Three early churns can be seen in the top cupboard section.

An Indian coverlet is placed over a Family Heirloom Weavers linen coverlet on the master bedroom bed.

Audrey uses the early table with red base in the corner as her writing desk.

A pair of swans carved by Danny Gregan, a local artist, fills the top shelf of a large wardrobe made of poplar. When Rich and Audrey purchased the wardrobe it was raining and the inside had just been painted. By the time they reached home, the paint had run down the sides and Rich was forced to redo the interior.

For information on The Rustique Antique business in Mendon, Pennsylvania, please call 724-872-5122. The shop is open 10-5 every day except Christmas, Easter, and Thanksgiving.

Chapter 2

Barbara and Michael Burnett

Barbara and Mike Burnett purchased their home on Ryker's Ridge, about four miles from Madison, Indiana, 18 years ago and took on a commitment to work hard and develop new hobbies! Barbara, a single mom with three boys, and Mike with one son have been married over 30 years. They lived in a new house in town and mentioned to the owner of their present home they were interested if the house ever came on the market. It did six months later and Barbara and Mike found themselves the proud owners of a brick 14-room, circa 1850 home which features a stone addition dating to the 1820's and a log cabin wing off the main house dating to the late 1700's. The logs on the cabin were covered with aluminum siding, which Barbara and Mike removed. Mike, a VP at Madison Hospital, was newly introduced to antiques by Barbara and had never built or remodeled anything. Since then

Mike and Barbara have done so much restoration and renovation that I was exhausted just hearing about it all. They consolidated rooms and removed others to create hallways and additional bathrooms, as well as removed all the new flooring and carpeting. Barbara's Dad and brother are carpenters and were able to help with much of the work.

The Burnett's used Old Village "Rittenhouse Ivory" for the exterior trim. An old sleigh with blue-green paint which Barbara fills with cedar trees during the holidays is protected on the porch of the cabin.

It appears that many buildings have been torn down on the property over the years, leaving what Barbara describes as "patios" in a number of spots, such as the side of the cabin. Mike built the arbor in the woods in the back.

Barbara filled a grape cart on one side of the front door and rested a flower-filled bucket on the other side. Note the unique oval transom window, original to the house.

Mike built a number of stacked split rail fences around the yard; one encloses an area in front of the cabin porch which holds a large variety of herbs.

Mike chipped off all the stucco which covered the original stone at the back of the house. The balcony porch is off the master bedroom.

Barbara and Mike have wondered if the house was originally a mill of some type, as the large grinding wheel came with the property. Seen also in the garden is the remnant of an old pump cover. The old bell, purchased at an auction by Barbara's Dad, was a gift to her from him.

Barbara said there are porches all around the house, such as this one off the utility room, which they believe was the original summer kitchen. An early chippy white painted pie safe holds a large bee skep. The twig bench is a swing.

The arbor seen at the end of the back porch is reached by a series of stone steps Mike built over the years. When previous owners tore down buildings, they left piles of stone everywhere, which Barbara and Mike have used in their gardens.

Barbara has filled an early cement washtub on iron legs with potted geraniums. Mike built the folk art log cabin shown alongside a bee skep, one of his developed new hobbies.

A concrete sheep overlooks some of the 11 acres that Mike and Barbara own. The property was completely wooded when they bought it. Wait till you see what they've added!

Barbara's 10' X 12' herb potting shed is one of three early log cabins Mike has built on the property.

They purchased it at an auction. A blue granite wash tub hangs on the side. Mike built the tin roof extension on the side to hold the bee skeps.

Inside, an early metal and wood rack used for drying herbs and fruit holds an old watering can, bee skep, and potted plant in the corner.

The second cabin belongs to Mike and dates to 1807. It provides a dual purpose. The first floor serves as his workshop and the second floor his space for antiques and collections.

Mike built the stone bench in front. The small bell which may have been a school bell was a gift to Mike from Barbara.

The second floor of Mike's cabin is filled with his collections of bear skin rugs, old muskets, Indian head arrows, and frontier items. Barbara said Mike can't sit still and doesn't play golf so he directs his energies to building and collecting. Barbara said when she puts something in the basement for storage from her collection, it often reappears in Mike's cabin.

Mike displays an early coonskin hat on the small child's bed in the corner. Leather pouches, powder horns, and snowshoes can be seen in the pictures above and left.

Mike's collection of Indian head arrows is displayed on the wall behind the table, set for the next meal.

The third cabin is Mike's fishing cabin. Mike built this cabin from logs found on the property. The large cement trough, which Barbara hauled home with the help of a friend and a farm wagon, functions as a container for water pouring from the old pump Mike built.

The original mantel in the living room was cement, which Barbara tore off to add the wooden mantel seen in the picture; it surrounds a coal burning stove. The settee and flame-stitch patterned chairs are from Johnston Benchworks and were purchased at a local country shop.

The 19thC jelly cupboard in original red paint was found in Lebanon, Ohio. Barbara is an avid collector of vintage Christmas items and stores some of them in the cupboard. The mustard base and old red painted breadboard top sawbuck table was found at auction.

The large stepback is also filled with holiday items. Barbara's great aunt made the quilt draped on the stack of early trunks with red paint.

The pie safe right retains its original tins with stars.

Barbara displays a small child's toy wagon inside a larger vintage wagon with paint. Barbara repainted all the walls in the house with a Benjamin Moore paint called "Moon Glow" when she redecorated throughout in black and mustard tones.

The large cupboard in red paint holds a television. Two of Mike's folk art cabins are displayed on top. A 19thC dough box in green paint rests on the raised stone hearth and holds magazines.

An old hay rake holds an assortment of baskets. Mike made the replica of their home and cabin seen at the left side of the mantel grouped with two early painted firkins.

The white shelf made by Sally Whims holds a collection of painted measures and an apple green carrier filled with balls of yarn. Barbara couldn't resist buying the hooked rug which resembles their home with the cabin addition to the side.

Barbara loves yellowware and displays some in the tall red cupboard with screen front, which was found in Waynesville, Ohio. A batter bowl stands on top. Barbara is particularly fond of the lidded butter crock on the first shelf and a rolling pin, a recent acquisition, on the second shelf down. An early candlebox with red wash hangs beside the cupboard.

Barbara has draped a vintage quilt over a chimney cupboard in mustard paint standing in the entrance into a small bathroom on the first floor.

Barbara likes the whimsical look of the vintage shower head found at a local flea market.

An early washstand holds a group of handmade soaps, a candlestick and a douter. Barbara used Olde Century paint "Olde Forge Mustard" in this room. Not shown is one of two claw foot tubs the Burnetts have in the house.

Barbara's kitchen counters are black-tinted concrete. She appreciates the ease of upkeep and feels that the counters add an aged look. An old drain board holds a wooden rack of drying yellowware plates. Banded yellowware crocks are displayed on an early dough board.

Barbara loves to collect old spice apothecaries or any pieces with small drawers. Two are seen in the kitchen. A coffee grinder is mounted on the window trim, while a large yellowware bowl holds butter molds and treen kitchenware. Barbara has owned these pieces for over 30 years, as she collected them when she couldn't afford anything else.

A new Hartland stove blends with the period, although Barbara deems the small oven totally inadequate when trying to cook for her family of 20.

The screened pie safe hangs over an old store counter which Barbara uses as her island. The pie display rack, which Barbara uses to show her cookie cutter, rolling pin, and tin collections, was a gift from her son and daughter-in-law.

A tin dough board and rolling pin hang over an old Jersey coffee bin in dry red paint.

Beside the stairway, an early church pew holds a vintage yellow and white quilt.

The stove is a salesman's sample and closely resembles the one in Barbara's kitchen

Barbara has filled the blue/gray painted screen pie safe with pieces of pottery. A granite blue meat grinder hangs on the wall above it. Three of Barbara's spice box collections surround a box containing marked spice tins.

The dining room area is off the kitchen and located in the log cabin addition. The rooster rug was made by Barbara's mother. The farm table was found in Waynesville, Ohio, while the chairs are Shaker found in Kentucky. Early dough bowls are seen in the center of the table beside an early red handled rolling pin and black homespun bonnet.

Tucked in the corner, a zinc-lined early dry sink in red paint holds butter presses and an early wooden bowl rack on which Barbara has placed two vintage blue bowls.

The early hanging plate rack holds a set of blue plates. A collection of blown glass tin-lidded jars is displayed in the dry sink found in Nashville at Heart of Country.

The chairs seen below were purchased at The Seraph. An early black flour sifter can be seen at the edge of the picture.

The large corner cupboard holds a collection of blue and white stoneware.

Barbara uses the large red jelly cupboard to hold all her baking products. She purchased the cupboard with thick white paint and dry scraped it down to the original red. Vintage aprons and clothing can be seen on the peg rack and door.

A large hanging pine screen pie safe is suspended from the beams over a standing dough box and collection of early bread boards and peels. Mike made the folk art houses on top of the cupboard which Barbara has decorated with bittersweet vines.

A large farm table in the utility room comes in handy when the entire family comes for a meal. Barbara and Mike think this was a summer kitchen and found evidence of it when they were remodeling. A shelf holds a collection of laundry room related tins. Vintage clothing hangs on a wooden hanging rack.

Deep window sills created by the house's thick stone walls provide ample space for more collections. Here on the utility room sill, Barbara has placed children's toys such as an ironing board, a Bissell sweeper, and a tin laundry tub.

This bedroom is found on the second floor of the log cabin addition; it was formerly two rooms which the Burnetts combined to accommodate the Sally Whims black bed.

Two early tool boxes are stacked at the foot of the bed. A small box containing four drawers is one of Barbara's favorites. A half corner cupboard can be seen beside a trundle bed reserved for Barbara and Mike's youngest grandson when he comes to visit.

A hallway leading from the cabin back to the main house is faced with original stone which Mike and Barbara uncovered when renovating.

Barbara used old red ticking to make the shams on the rope bed in one of the guestrooms.

Below, a bucket bench holds neatly folded textiles. A Sally Whims' shelf hangs above it and holds some of the Steif bears Barbara collects. More vintage textiles are seen in the opposite corner of the room in an early small pine cupboard.

A mustard painted cupboard hangs over the claw foot tub.

An old washboard acts as a tray on the tub.

The upstairs landing railing is perfect for hanging vintage quilts.

An assortment of painted boxes can be seen peeking over the top, while a plate rack by Sally Whims holds four painted dough bowls.

Barbara used a paint called "Meeting House Brown" on the trim in the master bedroom. Family Heirloom pillow covers and coverlet dress the bed made by Sally Whims.
A small blanket chest on legs holds early quilts.

An old basket on the cherry chest holds some of Barbara's small bear collection.

The washstand and pitcher and bowl, while not as early as other pieces in the house, hold special meaning to Barbara as they belonged to her grandmother.

I included the picture seen left because its simplicity reminds me of a Shaker scene.

The size of the Burnett's home, not to mention the extensive work they have done the last 18 years, makes me wonder how they have time to rest.

Chapter 3

Eileen and Peter Litwin

When I began *Marsh Homestead Country Antiques* in 1998, my shop was located in a small addition to the Northfield (Connecticut) General Store. Within two years I moved my shop to a large, finished, red barn building owned by Peter Litwin outside Litchfield, Connecticut. It made the perfect spot for my six-room shop, and I enjoyed the contact with Peter over the 2-1/2 years I rented space. Ten years later, I called Peter and his wife Eileen and asked if I could include their home in a book. Peter and Eileen's home was built circa 1765 by Captain Theodore Catlin; land records indicate that the road was laid in 1767 and the house was already there. Peter's grandparents came to the United States from Poland and purchased the farm in 1928. Peter is the third generation of Litwins to occupy the 265 acre farm, which he and Eileen purchased from Peter's parents in 1979. Both Peter's grandfather and father operated a dairy farm on the property that Peter's parents named Arbutus Farm after the proliferation of trailing arbutus on the stone ledges. Peter is a retired attorney and now pursues other interests such as carving birds, turning bowls and plates, and making furniture, while Eileen has retired her private massage therapy practice. Both love to travel and are always in search of additions to their eclectic collections.

The house is stained with Cabot's solid color stain "Red Tile", while the trim paint is Old Village "Tea Caddy Green". The millstone leaning against the front wall is one of many Peter has collected. It was purchased privately and came from an early mill in nearby Goshen, Connecticut.

The Litwin's magnificent gardens were featured in "Simply Country Gardens". The grounds display old stone pieces such as architectural fragments, well stones, and stone wheel pulleys that were part of 18thC life. Peter tired of painting the picket fence and trimming the bushes replaced now by the stone wall. Influenced by "crossovers" he had seen on trips to England and Ireland, Peter incorporated the stone steps which go through to the other side.

A crossover allows humans to cross from pasture to pasture while animals would not dare to try.

A large lye stone is placed by the side entrance. A bottomless barrel, filled with hardwood ash, would be placed on the stone, and water then poured into the ash; leached lye ran into the grooves and out the spout into a bucket. The lye was then boiled until thick enough to "float an egg" on the surface indicating it was ready to make soap. An early piece of granite, chiseled into a cylindrical tool, can be seen amidst the plants. A blacksmith yoke and handle make it possible to roll the cylinder.

Gate and hitching posts, found locally, stand beside two side entrances. The peaked stone is a capstone which would have been placed on a pier or monument; Peter has it resting on a stone post.

The front entrance is a large room. The Impressionistic painting by George Glenn Newell, well known in Litchfield County and Eastern New York State, depicts a pastoral scene with cows and appealed to Peter as a link with his family history. A pair of contemporary banister back chairs was crafted by Craig Farrow of Vermont.

The seat hooked rug pad, shown below, was fashioned by an artisan from Woodbury, Connecticut.

The lift-top six-board chest was purchased from Jeffrey Tillou of Litchfield. It is grain decorated with the 'tree of life' in the upper front panel and initialed on either side. Swags and tassel stencils adorn the front panel.

When the picture was taken I did not notice Claire, the Litwin's cat, as she blends beautifully with the rug. A male wood duck decoy, carved by Mark McNair, is seen on top of a drop leaf curly maple table with capriole legs purchased from Wayne Maddox of Woodbury, Connecticut. The landscapes were done by Litchfield artist Adelaide Deming.

Peter made the corner cupboard which holds a collection of blue Canton platters.

Beneath the Moravian star, a unique buggy whip holder has been placed on a metal stand offering an interesting spiritual appearance. The holder would have been fastened to a wall and the whips held by the finger-like extensions. The third shelf down holds an English cream ware jar featuring exquisite decoration. A decoy coot carved by Jim Keefer stands to its right. On the bottom shelf, far left, stands an English comb ware plate and, far right, a mocha pitcher.

A Wadsworth, Lounsbury, and Turner pillar and scroll mantel clock rests on a small shelf above a mustard paint-decorated dressing table. The milking stool beneath the table was a gift to the Litwins from Craig Farrow.

The Connecticut corner chair is one of a pair the Litwins own. This one stands beneath a hand-carved Herter's owl with glass eyes and a bear claw beak.

A pair of carved ruddy turnstone birds is mounted on driftwood.

The painting above the early architectural mantel from a Hudson River Valley home is a signed Herb Abrams' painting of spring forsythia, a subject he painted once a year. This painting was his last and largest and includes over 200 shades of yellow. Carved Common Teals by Ken Gleason flank the painting. A large blue heron carving by the late Harold Corbin stands in the corner beneath an iron cresset-the bottom point of the cresset would have been driven into a pole or pipe and the top then forms a basket. Tree knots were placed in the basket and ignited. The primitive lighting illuminated a ship's bow to assist spear fishing.

The large stag is an original piece by J.W. Fiske Ironworks and acquired from the personal collection of Harold Corbin. A Herter's owl decoy is perched in the corner.

In 1981, Peter purchased the set of five black ducks, carved by Ken Gleason, then mortised and mounted each on a piece of butternut.

The barn swallow in full flight was carved from a single block of wood and presents an engaging point of interest.

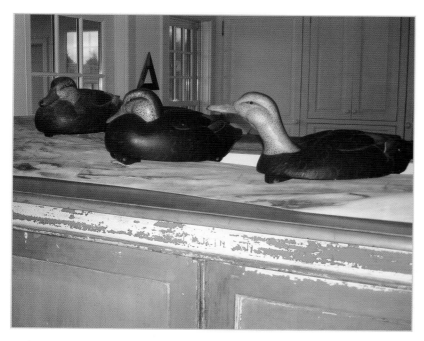

Walking down the hallway to the first floor master bedroom, a visitor encounters a gallery of early Grenfell rugs. Peter appreciates the simplicity and color of the pieces and has acquired a great variety.

A grain-painted six-board chest is predominantly displayed in the master bedroom. The curly maple four-poster bed is early.

A Grenfell rug depicting ducks in flight hangs above the headboard.

The early shorebird stands in front of a watercolor titled "Peter's Barn".

The apple green chest was purchased from a dealer in Connecticut and appealed to the Litwins because of the strong paint; it holds a simple green box with snipe hinges. The Impressionistic painting by Curtis Hanson blends beautifully with the green tones.

The Blackhawk horse weathervane horse is copper.

The kitchen is done with an English paint the Litwins discovered on a trip abroad. Peter applied a light brown wax to create an aged appearance.

The canisters are new pieces marked "Over and Back Yellowware" on the bottom. The backsplash tiles were custom-painted to represent each flower found on the property.

A detailed Victorian bud vase, found at Brimfield, enjoys a place of prominence on the island.

An early sheet iron peace dove weathervane creates a striking silhouette. Peter saw the piece years ago and didn't purchase it. Years later, it reappeared at a Colorado auction and he was able to purchase it with a phone bid. The rooster is a period piece which Peter placed to face east in the breakfast room. The pine table features a single-board top and a mustard painted base; it was purchased at the Hartford Antique Show. The matched set of hoop back Windsor chairs with mustard paint were crafted by Stephen Bedard.

Peter made the corner cupboard displayed with Blue Canton plates and hand-blown chestnut bottles. Small handmade decoy weights are barely visible on the ends of the shelves. The Summer Plover on top is early and originates from Willie Mayhew's in Edgartown on Martha's Vineyard, Massachusetts.

Peter uses the area above the window to display part of an extensive collection of early fishing bobbers.

Peter built the stepback which holds a variety of Blue Canton patterned platters. On top rests a knotted stick . . . someone in the early life of a white pine tree tied the central trunk in a knot . . . and it continued to grow that way.

Peter carves a variety of birds, some of which are seen below.

The 'circle of friends' candleholder was a gift from friends and was made in Central America.

The contemporary table in the formal dining room features a Sycamore, single-board top, while the trestle base is curly maple.

The paintings, below left, are indicative of the Litwin's eclectic tastes; as Peter says, he buys what appeals to him, without concern if a piece fits with another. The representation of a chicken was purchased in Wyoming while Peter was on a fishing trip; he chose it because of the Impressionistic style and strong green paint. The painting of pomegranates was purchased along the Seine.

A period goose decoy carved by Joe Lincoln stands on top of a green-painted two-drawer chest with lift top purchased privately.

An oil on canvas depicting peaches hangs above a mustard three-drawer dressing table with delightful paint decorations.

The large 19thC stepback with strong color was purchased from Jeffrey Tillou of Litchfield. Peter made the large cherry burl bowl displayed on the shelf. The set of graduated tin heart molds was found at Gilyard Antiques in Litchfield.

A period Connecticut landscape hangs over the Sheraton curly maple bed in the first floor guestroom.

A bull weathervane stands in front of a curly maple Chippendale mirror with scallops.

The painting over the mantel is a Nesbit. A yoke back arm chair can be seen at the edge of the picture, while Philadelphia brass andirons and a fender enclose the hearth.

A Seth Thomas pillar and scroll mantel clock with wooden gears hangs above a Wallace Nutting sunflower chest, so named because of its carved sunflower heads; it is a true replica of a piece in the Deerfield, Massachusetts, museum.

The guestroom upstairs is decorated in tones of soft greens and pink. The unique salmon grain painted chest was found in Plymouth, Connecticut. Peter is aware that a few other pieces exist with similar surface and hopes to find another.

Peter groups a collection of Frank Benson black and white etchings, some of which recently appeared in "Frank W. Benson's Etchings, Drypoints, and Lithographs", by John Ordeman.

Isn't the early skunk hooked rug wonderful? It was purchased at the Wilton Antique Show in Wilton, Connecticut, and is featured over a four drawer butternut chest.

The Litwin's guest powder room is whimsical! Peter used birch bark to face the cabinet and create some of the frames.

He fashioned the stencils from ferns and tree leaves found on the property and then stenciled the walls with a variety of green tones.

The woodcock was carved by Ken Gleason.

Many partners defer the decorating, and likewise, my husband, Jeff, accedes the decorating to me. He will be the first to say that he always likes the results and trusts my opinion. "That's your department."

I asked Peter how Eileen feels about their décor. Peter first responded that she appreciates what he likes . . . then fine-tuned his reply to, "She tolerates my tastes." Peter affectionately remarked, "Eileen collects and cultivates friendships." Their home, impeccably decorated throughout with stimulating pieces, old and new, is obviously a joint venture.

Chapter 4

Maria and Rickey Walker

Just imagine how hard life must be for Maria Walker – her husband Rickey drags her off to antique shops every chance he gets! Rickey and Maria, both natives of Upstate New York, built their 4000 plus square foot home in Middletown, Delaware, 12 years ago when they were transferred from Rickey's job with Met Life Insurance Company. Maria stayed behind in New York while their children finished school, while Rickey lived in a Delaware apartment and occupied his spare time exploring antique shops in Pennsylvania. By the time the house was finished and Maria and the children joined Rickey, he had already scoped out the best antique shops and couldn't wait to show Maria. Rickey is now a diehard antique collector who could spend every minute on the hunt, sometimes to the extent that Maria has to beg off because of other commitments. Maria had previously collected what she refers to as "cutesy country" prior to Rickey's new found pastime; now their home is filled with huge collections, antique smalls, and larger contemporary pieces, many of which Rickey has built. As if it's not enough for Maria to have to spend endless hours shopping, Rickey is forever asking her, "What do you want me to make now?"!

The large Tavern Room at the end of the house was a later addition and reflects Maria and Rickey's interest in historic Williamsburg, Virginia. The Rumford fireplace fills nearly the entire wall. In fact, the mason declared that he didn't think there was a larger chimney in all of Delaware! Maria says that they live in this room; they use the fireplace often for cooking and appreciate the room's size when entertaining. The sawbuck table was built with reclaimed wood. The two ladderback chairs, seen at the end of the table, came from one of the first five homes built in Delaware.

Maria and Rickey use lots of color throughout the house. All the rooms are painted with Benjamin Moore paint – this room with a color called "Golden Hurst". A large pewter oval

platter, purchased in Yorktown, Virginia, is flanked on the mantel by two large chargers. The mantel was removed from a 19thC barn in Pennsylvania. Hanging beside a utensil holder with herbs, a rare small iron rod holds a set of utensils created for a small child. Beside it hangs an early fly catcher.

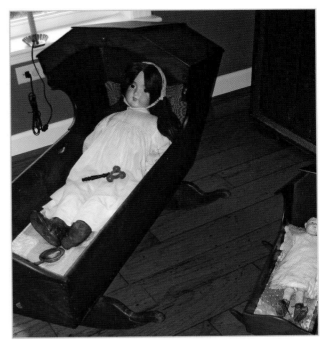

Maria and Rickey purchased many of their large pieces at a shop in New Jersey; many were made by Good Intent Farm of Pennsylvania – the red sugar chest to the right of the fireplace is one example. Above it, a tavern sign painted by Kathy Graybill is one of many Rickey and Maria display throughout the house. The blue standing butter churn was purchased at Yellow Garage Antiques in Mullica Hill, New Jersey. The stepback , another piece made by Good Intent Farm, stands to the left of the fireplace and holds pieces of Olde World Pewter, as well as salt-glazed stoneware on top.

On the floor in front of the cupboard, Maria has placed two early cradles – the larger of the two was purchased at Royal Port Antiques in New Jersey; it holds an 1890's Armand Marseille German bisque doll. Notice the antique rattle Maria has placed in the doll's lap. The smaller cradle is also an antique but the doll a newer piece. Maria has tucked a small fabric mouse with an antique mousetrap next to the fireplace.

Rickey made the bowl rack which hangs above the red dry sink from Good Intent Farm. Maria believes she has over 300 pieces of redware in her collection,; most from David T. Smith or Greg Schooner.

The table in front of the window is a hutch table which Maria and Rickey use when not entertaining. The corner cupboard, filled with more Olde World Pewter was made by Rickey. A Kathy Graybill tavern sign hangs above an early sewing cabinet that Rickey painted after removing the machine; it is now used as a sideboard.

A grouping in the opposite corner provides a quiet spot for conversation. The Windsor chairs are from Lawrence Crouse. The candlestand with pie crust top is early.

The living room is painted with a paint called "Hot Apple Spice". All of the upholstered furniture is from Johnston Benchworks. Rickey made the coffee table and two end tables in the living room. A painting titled Reverend Walker Skating hangs above one of the tables.

Maria tucked an early trunk filled with contemporary dolls beneath a Kathy Graybill sign in the corner. A reproduction painting showing a mother and her twins hangs over the camelback sofa.

Two butter churns are seen on either end of the Lawrence Crouse bench which holds a collection of dolls. The churn on the left is a Rowe pottery piece from the historical collection.

The dining room is painted with Benjamin Moore "Yellow Oxide "paint. Portraits titled Mr. and Mrs. Pierce hang on either side of a bowl rack made by Rickey and filled with redware plates. The table and chairs are Lawrence Crouse.

Maria keeps the tree in the corner up year- round; it displays a collection of redware ornaments.

Rickey made the cupboard seen left . He finishes most of his pieces with Barn Red paint over black to create an aged look.

A large family room connects with the kitchen at the back of the house. The room features a cathedral ceiling and raised hearth fireplace against one entire wall.

Seen above left is the family room looking down from the loft hallway on the second floor.

A child's chair, once used in Maria's gift shop which she owned many years ago, holds a doll on the raised hearth. The picture over the mantel is a print of a quilt square but so intricate that it fools many guests into thinking it is an antique piece. The redware plate of two birds in the center is the first plate done in that pattern by Crocker and Springer.

The paint in the family room is called "Hillcrest Tan". Good Intent Farm made the dry sink which holds a Williamsburg blue and white punch bowl set.

Olde World Pewter fills the shelves of the hutch cupboard Rickey made.

Maria displays a collection of George Washington china, in a glass-front Good Intent Farm *hutch*. A document box, painted in the Rufus Porter style by Kathy Graybill is tucked beneath.

Maria's kitchen is painted with a color called "Philipsburg Blue". A stack of graduated benches stands at the end of a combination working island and counter for eating. Maria and Rickey own over 30 Windsor chairs six of which surround the contemporary table in the informal dining area. Rickey built shelves, similar to that over the dining area window, over all windows in the house to allow additional display space.

The den is painted with a color called "Alligator Green". Maria displays the feather tree ,decorated with a variety of fabric bird ornaments, all year long in memory of her mother's love for birds.

Hanging above the sofa is one of Maria's favorite pieces; a King Solomon's Temple sampler found in Pennsylvania; it is signed Caroline Price and dated 1846.

A large reproduction black desk holds the beginnings of Maria's newest collection – old school bells.

A flock of sheep appears to be meandering across the table in front of the window.

Maria has done the master bedroom in tones of mustard and black. the paint is "Golden Hurst". The trunk at the foot of the bed is old, while the hooked rug depicting a horse weathervane is a new piece.

A settee and chair at one end of the room provide a quiet area for reading and watching television.

A wire tree on the coffee table holds a variety of small wooden birds.

One of the four guestrooms is painted with "Hot Apple Spice" paint. A Lawrence Crouse bed with mustard paint is covered with a contemporary quilt of reds and sage greens.

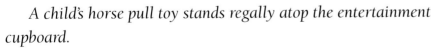

A child's horse pull toy stands regally atop the entertainment cupboard.

A second guestroom, painted in "Yellow Oxide" paint, is furnished with a black turned high post bed and a settee bench.

A reproduction black Shaker tall clock in the foyer holds Rickey and Maria's granddaughter Hailey's tea set . . . which she and Maria use on special occasions.

To my thinking, Rickey and Maria's home is a perfect example of how we country collectors can tastefully blend new and old pieces to create a warm reflection of our personalities and tastes.

Chapter 5

✦ ❋ ✦

Sandra and Gordon Mariner

Sandra and Gordon Mariner married 41 years ago and have collected since the very first. Gordon owns a company called *Ad Art Signs*; he also possesses a talent for crafting furniture. Sandra, a retired mail carrier, once owned a gift shop and was able to purchase wholesale many of their pieces. The fact that Gordon could build furniture and create display pieces for Sandra's shop was a real plus. Problem was, every time Gordon made a piece, Sandra priced it high – and it sold anyway! They have two grown children and four grandchildren who

now occupy their time, but Sandra has entertained the distant thought of perhaps opening another shop someday. Gordon and Sandra moved to their 1850's colonial in 2002 from a home which Gordon had built. They have been forced to raise their present house twice to replace its foundation, and learned from a contractor that in 1949 the home was moved 14 miles to its present location.

Old photographs show their home in its original location and condition.

Sandra likes to mix old and new pieces, many of which carried over from her days as a shop owner, such as the hanging folk art doll in the entranceway. The slant top desk is early and one of Sandra's favorite pieces. Gordon made the plate rack above which holds two newer redware plates and an older plate seen on the far right.

The large print seen above was purchased at the Waterfowl Festival in nearby Easton, Maryland; it is a numbered print entitled, "What's You Looking At?" Gordon remade the sideboard server from an old piece and refinished it to give it an aged look. The early fiddleback chair in the corner is one of a pair given to Sandra by a friend.

A small water closet is tucked under the stairway in the front hall. I included this picture because the peach towels blend so beautifully with the rosy peach cheeks of the folk art angel above. The white molding with chippy paint serves as the angel's stylized wings.

A beautifully framed collage consists of the treasures that Sandra's mother's great-grandparents used for their wedding. The groom's ascot serves as the background for the bride's gloves and purse.

Sandra inherited the large sofa with wooden trim and had it reupholstered in a Wedgewood blue pattern. A local shop upholstered the settee in the corner to match. Sandra used a paint called "Khaki" throughout the house.

The dry sink in the corner is old and was used in Sandra's shop as a display piece. Surrounding it is a grouping of sketches, watercolors, and a few samplers done by a friend. The demi-lune table is a newer piece, perhaps Canadian.

The large two-piece glass front stepback was purchased locally from a dealer who bought it for his home . . . but couldn't fit it through his door. Sandra has placed a magnolia garland and a large crow on top. The camelback sofa came from Sandra's shop, while Gordon made the shelf above it. The large table and Windsor chairs are new.

Gordon used an old door to create the front of the server; the apron back is a thick board which Gordon took from an old table.

The chest in blue came from a shop in Snow Hill, Maryland, where Sandra grew up.

Gordon and Sandra totally remodeled the kitchen as part of the yearlong renovations when they moved into the house. The table is one that the construction grew used as a worktable and that Gordon cut down and converted into the kitchen farm table. Sandra's countertops are granite and her floor stone tile. A collection of decorative 'cat' plates is displayed above the stove.

Sandra angles the kitchen table slightly so that the dining room and kitchen tables do not line up like a train.

The large white dining room cabinet is a married piece that Gordon built. Sandra said it is heavy as lead and one reason why she doesn't move things around in her house. Where it goes, it stays. The pie safe retains its original tins and was a piece from Gordon's family.

Sandra has decorated the family room in salmon tones. The jelly cupboard is old; Gordon added the apron. The clock is a reproduction. The whimsical bird on the wall was a gift from a friend. The chest in front of the sofa is an early piece that Gordon restored and refinished.

The large landing at the top of the stairs provides a quiet area for reading. The "Khaki" trim paint accents the black, which Sandra carried over in the toile fabric on the chair and the stencils.

Sandra continued the use of the "Khaki" and black in the small bathroom off the landing; the curtains are black and white check although hard to discern. Gordon made the black shelf that holds a collection of lidded glass jars. The apothecary just inside the door is a new piece.

Gordon made the black pencil-post bed with the understanding that if Sandra didn't like it, she could sell it. Obviously she liked it! They purchased the large chest of drawers at an antique shop on their travels.

A pristine quilt, purchased at a local furniture store, decorates the bed in the guestroom.

The large wardrobe, also in black, is a new piece purchased at a local country shop.

Sandra and Gordon were in the process of landscaping their back patio area when I visited; I was able to capture a few pictures of their koi pond tucked in the corner of the yard.

Chapter 6

Carol and George Meekins

Carol and George Meekins are the owners of *Country Treasures* in Preston, Maryland, a business they have owned for 31 years specializing in 18th and 19thC American country painted furniture. In addition to operating a shop full time, they also participate in a number of shows throughout the United States. They were traveling to a show when they passed a small "For sale" sign on a property owned by an elderly couple. On the return trip, the sign had been replaced by a Realtor's sign and Carol and George purchased the property. That was in 1996 and, as George says, they began their "five year plan" restoring the heating, electrical, plumbing etc. Their contractor happens to be their best friend and worked diligently on every detail. The house featured lap siding – too far gone to repair or cover – so George and Carol used 30,000 18th C handmade, (some bricks retain fingerprints) Flemish bond style bricks to cover the house and restore the fireplaces. George began by repairing and restoring furniture and then collected and stored so many pieces that Carol and George were forced to open a shop. While they used to work with about a dozen pickers throughout the United States, they now prefer to do their own buying and focus entirely on painted pieces, which they started to collect in the mid 1980's.

The 19thC portrait in the parlor appealed to George because of its unusual depiction of a woman wearing a bow tie. George and Carol used Williamsburg "Wyatt House Gold", a neutral color that blends with the individual colors in the room. Four boxes are stacked beneath the portrait. Carol has a passion for early boxes and blanket chests. The white scalloped chest was found in North Carolina while the box beneath it in Virginia. George and Carol left the floor painted its original pewter gray.

The glass front corner cupboard in apple green dates to circa 1820. A collection of Flow Blue and Staffordshire is displayed with a unique Oriental 1000 Butterflies plate similar to one seen on the Antique Road Show recently. Hanging on the wall above another small stack of miniature blanket chests is a late 18thC/early 19thC lollipop painted New England wallbox. The oil on canvas is mid 19thC and depicts a flock of sheep. A small tiger maple and walnut blue splay-legged table with original base was found in Pennsylvania.

George and Carol said the blue base tavern table dates to the early 18thC and is the oldest piece they own. It features a pin top that enables the top to be removed for either serving or cleaning, and was found in the Hudson Valley, New York area. An early New England rush light stands on top.

In the corner, a six-panel 18thC cupboard in pastel yellow holds one of George and Carol's favorite pieces, a blue-green dovetailed miniature blanket chest; both were found in Delaware.

George gave Carol the Pennsylvania, 100% original green small hutch table as an anniversary gift. It could have been a salesman's sample but more likely was created as a toy for a child.

In the foyer, George and Carol have placed the Pennsylvania tiger maple apothecary found at a local auction; it retains its original salmon paint and hand-dovetailed craftsmanship throughout. Charles Joiner of Chestertown, Maryland, carved the decoy.

The oil painting was found in Upstate New York by George and his son. They traveled to Syracuse to make a delivery and were unable to find a room anywhere. After taking shelter in a hospital waiting room, they found the painting the next day at auction.

How's this for a picture? The vibrant blue pie safe was covered in thick white paint when George and Carol found the Kentucky piece in Texas. The tins with pewter gray patina resemble samplers. The North Carolina Spanish brown walnut table dates to circa 1820. The chairs are early bowback Windsors of New England origin. A yellow trencher holds a large wax arrangement created by Doris Stauble of Wiscasset, Maine. A spectacular blue basket can be seen atop the 1810 hanging red painted corner cupboard found in New Hampshire. George found the signed stag weathervane with the original label in Philadelphia. Two stacks of small Shaker pantry boxes, one round and one oval, are seen on the left side of the mantel.

A pair of wooden carved folk art pieces stands on the hearth beside a blue painted basket. The man's hat comes off to reveal hair made of cotton. The clothing is also entirely handmade.

A superb pair of wax folk art figures holds a place of prominence on the mantel.

The lollipop handled wallbox in blue paint is a late 18C New England piece featuring pinstripe feather paint on all four sides. Beneath the hanging corner cupboard, small blanket chests in graduated sizes from Pennsylvania and Delaware are stacked. The ladderback is from Massachusetts and retains its original blue paint.

The hanging cupboard in blue is entirely hand-dovetailed. It hangs above a blue work table holding a sugar cone and pewter plate. The corner cupboard was found on the Eastern Shore of Delaware and dates to the mid 18thC; it features original glass and H hinges. Its blue paint with raised panels in white typifies that region. Carol uses it to display her large collection of spongeware. Three baskets on top were made in Delmar, Delaware, so named because half the town is located in Delaware and the other half in Maryland. The baskets are done in three colors and date to the mid-late 19thC.

The red dry sink was found in Pennsylvania and is crafted with two overhanging drawers typical of the York County region. George and Carol's son Robert, who works in the business, found the bittersweet painted large compote. The two portraits tell the story of a poacher who sets his bait in the first painting and is seen at sunrise having caught a rabbit in the second.

The Meekins painted their kitchen Williamsburg "Powell Walker Red". The blue-gray island is an old Pennsylvania store counter dating to the 19thC. George built an insert, comprised of drawers and cupboards, to fill the entire open side in back. The cupboard doors are affixed with reproduction rat tail hinges. Two bail handled pantry boxes are stacked beside the Vermont soapstone farm sink. A Jersey coffee bin serves as a trash receptacle. Assorted stools add more color.

George and Carol couldn't resist the strong blue of the three-drawer Delaware jelly cupboard which they've placed in the adjoining kitchen eating area. A Midwest still life painting of fruit was chosen for its strong colors as well. The table with apple green painted base was found in Virginia and holds a large beehive bowl from upstate New York. A child's chair with blue paint found in Pennsylvania stands in front of the window. The glass front corner cupboard was found in North Carolina but is a Pennsylvania piece. It is unique in that the top door is hung opposite from the bottom. Three painted baskets are displayed on top. The middle red basket with blue handle was a birthday gift to Carol from George.

The sign seen above was a gift from a friend. The collection of stoneware butter churns is displayed on a bench with red wash. The churns were all made by Peter Herman of Baltimore, Maryland, during the 1870's. The small blue apothecary from Bucks County, Pennsylvania, is one of the first pieces George and Carol ever purchased.

The small blue lidded box was found in Pennsylvania and hangs above a chrome yellow

painted box which holds an early turned bowl. The large early 19thC cupboard is made of yellow and white pine and is a Chester County, Pennsylvania piece. It was purchased at auction and is actually a pie safe stepback. The bottom is black, the top red, the sides are red with black sponge painting while the molding on top is black.

The end of the room is divided by a dry sink bucket bench; it features open drawers and no bottom. Stacks of early painted pantry boxes fill the well.

The early green painted horse on the mantel is oversized and was an anniversary present.

In the hallway leading to the mudroom, a crock cupboard found near Gettysburg, Pennsylvania, has a dovetailed case and dry red paint. The folk art watermelon slice was a gift from a friend. Each green painted measure in the stack is stamped Sampson, Carol's maiden name. Isn't the 18thC lantern with blue paint gorgeous?

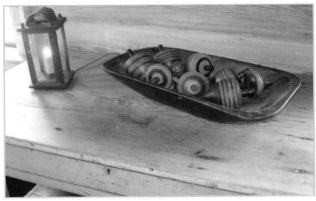

And speaking of gorgeous . . . the early 19thC blue apothecary was found in Pennsylvania. George didn't care that it had one drawer darker than the others. It is what it is! The patriotic hooked rug was purchased at Skinner's auction house in Boston.

This is the mudroom! George and his son Craig drew and stenciled the floor; they chose green and mustard rather than the usual black and white to bring more color into the room. The apple green table is 18thC and has splay legs and two drawers; it was found in the Virginia Shenandoah Valley. It originally had a mustard base and was dry scraped down. Carol purchased the small wheelbarrow on top at a show because the side is painted "Preston", the town where they live. The old pine pie safe in the back was purchased and refinished by the Meekins in the 1960's.

Found in Lancaster County, Pennsylvania, the pumpkin paint corner cupboard with green interior and door retains its original glass.

An early lantern found in North Carolina and a painted trencher sit on a table with pretty pastel yellow paint, while a collection of early tops fills the trencher.

A contemporary Jefferson writing chair in blue, shown above right, is perhaps an early copy of a Wallace Nutting.

Three baskets are displayed on top of the large glass front secretary that Carol uses as her desk. It features an arch apron front and is made of southern heart pine; the secretary is from Virginia and was used in a printers shop during the Civil War.

George and Carol use the base of an early blue painted corner cupboard to create a vanity in the guest bathroom off the mudroom. Hanging on the wall to the left is an early wooden piece of a plate rack with blue paint which George and Carol have repurposed as a towel rack.

George and Carol were in the process of creating a patriotic theme on the glass enclosed porch off the back of the house. The project was a work-in-progress when I visited but still worthy of sharing the beautiful pieces which George and Carol had already placed. The six-panel large wardrobe fills one end of the room; it features strong blue paint, dates to the 1820's, and was found in Maryland. A zinc lined apple washer table in blue paint was found in Upstate New York.

The Centennial 13 star flag was a gift from their son and once flew over nearby Easton, Maryland. A single-drawer splay legged table from Pennsylvania has a deep apron, single board top, and ogee molded edges on four sides.

A boat model, signed on the back "Oxford, Maryland", was purchased from a friend's collection. It stands on a blue painted six-board chest.

The bed seen left in one of the guestrooms is a Pennsylvania red painted piece from the Federal era, circa 1820. The bed table was one of the first pieces the Meekins purchased. The wonderful hooked rug above the bed reads Welcome in Our Home rather than Welcome to Our Home.

Carol uses coverlets as bed linens to create a canopy on the contemporary bed. A blue five- drawer French footed chest was found in Pennsylvania and holds a vinegar painted box with Carol's initials on top.

George gave the large Noah's Ark, found in North Carolina, to Carol as a gift. It is filled with wooden animals and stands on a Federal blue chest found on the Eastern Shore of Maryland.

A delightful folk art painting by Robert Roebuck is one of a pair Carol couldn't pass up.

The third floor of the house is divided in half . . . his and hers. Carol added early laundry accessories – such as the scrub board with blue paint, the miniature wash tub, and the tiny washboard on the wall.

Carol keeps a hidden room – which she has yet to let her three year-old granddaughter know about. It will be a "coming of age" when Carol opens the door to her at some point in the future. A farmhand's bed in blue paint was found in Virginia. The wingback chair was made by a Pennsylvania cabinet maker and holds an early bear.

The miniature green cupboard was most likely a child's toy. A built-in shelf displays a walnut miniature tilt-top table, miniature boxes, and a stack of miniature painted stools.

George's side of the third floor is filled with his decoy collection.

I was surprised to learn that the small decoy seen below is actually made of rock and was created by son Robert as a child.

An advertising sign at the end of the room was a gift from Robert to George.

Country Treasures, located in Preston, Maryland, is open 7 days Monday–Saturday, 9–5, and Sunday, noon to 5. The shop contains 6500 square feet of beautifully displayed 18th and 19thC painted pieces. The Meekins maintain a website, www.mycountrytreasures. com and can be reached by phone at 410-673-2603. In addition to their shop, George and Carol also participate in shows in Brimfield, Nashville, York, Round Top, and Raleigh.

Chapter 7

Carolyn Carter

Carolyn Carter and her late husband Fred enjoyed antiquing and often compromised on the items they collected. Carolyn preferred primitives with early paint and Fred leaned toward a more finished surface with a stain. They usually traveled in a Corvette while antiquing and spent much time returning to pick up the pieces! After Fred died in 1995, Carolyn returned to Ironton, the town in southern Ohio where she grew up to purchase what she calls a "box house". Although the property deed indicates the house was built in 1925, Carolyn suspects it dates to an earlier period as the foundation appears to be older and many of the surrounding homes date to the 1830's. Carolyn worked 35 years for Sears Roebuck as an executive in the Customer Relations department and now works part-time as a receptionist for a CPA. Moving from a 2800 square foot home to a 900 square foot home meant choices had to be made. As a result Carolyn's home is filled with exquisite pieces which blend and fit perfectly into her limited space.

Carolyn enjoys gardening and completed all the landscaping herself. She employs help now to complete the gardening chores that require a stronger hand. In front, the garden area is enclosed with a handmade twig fence which Carolyn says lasts about two years.

A simple clear glass jar filled with Shasta daisies and coreopsis creates a wispy country look on the porch.

Carolyn loves primitive style birdhouses with tin roofs; her favorite is shown on the pole, right.

The house on the ground, below right, is called a toad house and isn't intended for birds. It was made by a local artisan.

Carolyn had always dreamed of having a log cabin but settled on the interior of the house finished to offer a log cabin effect.

Six years ago, Carolyn purchased an old barn and utilized the 140 year-old boards throughout her home. After she power washed them in scalding hot water three times, the boards were ready to be used in the house for floors, walls, and ceilings.

Carolyn began collecting almost 50 years ago and was influenced by a nearby farm where furniture was built on-site. Carolyn remembers visiting the farm as a 10 year-old child and listening to her uncle tell stories of early farm life while they sat on the porch swing. On the left side of the mantel is a long handle with a metal pan on the end. Carolyn recalls as a child holding the pan over the fire to warm milk. The portrait was purchased in Waynesville, Ohio, and dates to circa 1840. Some of Carolyn's extensive collection of hogscrapers and early candleholders is displayed on the mantel. The box on the far left of the mantel is an old document box with green paint and snipe hinges and rests beside McGuffey Readers used in Appalachia. The early 19thC hanging candle holder was used to hold rush lights. The table behind the settee is a New England table brought to Ohio by a picker. It features one drop-leaf similar to a baker's table and retains its original red paint. It is constructed with rose head nails and dates to the early 19thC. Carolyn found the early trencher in Newark, Ohio.

The spinning wheel is all original and purchased in New Hampshire from a family whose ancestors had owned it for generations. The spinning wheel was rumored to have been from the Civil War period when the family migrated from Manassas, Virginia, to Ohio. An early loom light is seen hanging from the side.

The primitive cupboard in the corner is constructed with rosehead nails. Each H hinge is unique. Carolyn remembers her uncle telling her that every room should have a corner cupboard.

The gorgeous Federal blue cupboard seen above was purchased from a noted dealer in Ohio. Three bowls – red, white, and blue – are displayed on the first shelf. The other shelves hold early small baskets and painted pantry boxes.

The small wall shelf to the left is an early carrier. The book on top is early and entitled "The Toy Shop – The Story of Lincoln". Leather bound books fill the first shelf. The sawbuck table below is one of four sawbucks Carolyn owns. This one is early mustard over blue and has a trough below.

An early apple box and canvas goose can be seen on top of the mustard cupboard found in Ohio. Two bail-handled pantry boxes with blue/green paint blend with the two smaller boxes of the same color above.

A wonderful early 19thC lift top New England dry sink with blue paint holds a leather-bound copy of "The History of Scioto County". Carolyn found the dark green painted wooden piece for $20 and immediately saw it as a repurposed candleholder which now hangs above the dry sink.

Hanging in the stairwell, a blue 17thC cupboard is constructed with rose head nails and early butterfly hinges.

A stoneware crock dresses each step on the stairs. The top three are from Carolyn's family; most of the other crocks were purchased for $40 or less.

The settle resting against the opening into the dining room is a barrel back from Maine.

Carolyn purchased the three-board top sawbuck table with red base because of the unique pin seen at the bottom of the picture. Carolyn believes it is a married piece dating to the mid to late 18thC. A treenware compote holds a bunch of grapes. Two treenware plates and horn cups complete the setting.

The four-slat chair is an early Amish piece and initialed on the back. It was found near Columbus, Ohio, and features a seat woven with a ribbon loom. The candlestand is Hudson Valley; it is all wood-pegged and retains early paint on the base.

An early grain bin in the back corner has red paint which her late husband refinished, and features breadboard ends and the original hinges.

Sitting on top of the table is an early make-do made from a log from a log home. The iron candleholder is early 18thC.

The hanging cupboard dating to the early 19thC was purchased in Newark, Ohio. A large treen dishpan from Texas is warped from the water and sun. The standing gooseneck iron candleholder was made by a tinsmith in Tipp City, Ohio, as were all the lighting pieces throughout the house.

An early green bowl with wonderful tin repairs hangs on the wall beside a reproduction black wall shelf. The box on the shelf is an early slide top candlebox beside an early leather-bound ledger.

The cupboard above right is referred to as a Missouri cupboard; Carolyn purchased it for $65 about 30 years ago. It retains its original tins and Carolyn has filled it with blue and white stoneware and a spatterware pitcher on the bottom shelf. The lidded pot in the center is an early Boston Beans pot.

Large dough bowls with paint fill the cupboard in the dining room corner. The white bowl on top is hand-turned and most likely dates to the 18thC. The large mustard bowl on the bottom shelf was found in New York.

Carolyn used some of the early barn boards to finish the walls in the kitchen to create a primitive appearance. The lollipop candlebox to the left of the sink retains its original dark green paint.

The cant-sided box with original red wash on the counter holds treen utensils and a unique swan butter press.

A long black spice box holds a sugar cone and early sugar nippers.

The early scrubber seen hanging on the cupboard front is made from hickory wood and was purchased at a show in Lebanon, Ohio.

An early lantern and two graduated pantry boxes are silhouetted on the hanging buttery against the window over the sink.

The cupboard made from barn boards conceals Carolyn's refrigerator.

A black hanging cupboard that Carolyn purchased over 30 years ago hangs over the stove that Carolyn uses daily. A large tin cooker seen in the foreground would have hung from the trammel in the fireplace and been used for cooking. A screen in the bottom catches the grease before it reaches the flames.

Carolyn displays some of her blue banded yellowware on a 20" wide shelf which came from the barn that she purchased. The wood planks on the floor were acquired from an Amish village near Columbus and measure as wide as 18".

The dry sink, made of poplar or pine, was purchased for $65 years ago and may have had the doors replaced.

The pine drop leaf table dates to the mid 19thC. A mold of bees wax covered with cheese cloth stands in the center on an early peel.

A variety of early baskets hang from the over 200 year old beams. A large trencher in the dry sink was purchased on one of Carolyn's travels in Tennessee. A doughbox with red paint was found in Ohio and stands on a Kentucky jelly cupboard under the window.

The two-tier candlebox in Spanish brown paint holds candles on the side of a tall mustard cupboard. Two unique pieces of yellowware with green can be seen on top.

Carolyn converted a small closet into a buttery off the kitchen, and thought it the perfect place to display an early butter churn. The top shelf holds an early flour box in dark green paint and in the shadows another butter churn in red. Vintage aprons hang on the peg ready for use.

The four-poster bed was found in Kentucky and dates to the Civil War era. The black rocker at the foot of the bed retains the original hand-painted horn of plenty on the back. In front of the window is a standing six-board dowry chest. A piece of Lindsey Woolsey is draped across the bottom of the bed.

A large 19thC cupboard in dry red wash and single wide door holds a folded stack of early quilts. The two quilts on top are pre-Civil War.

The comb seen right would have been used to create a ribbon weave similar to the one on the ladderback chair in Carolyn's dining room.

Carolyn used more of the early barn boards to line the walls in the bathroom. The dry blue-gray cupboard is much more interesting than a medicine cabinet. The scalloped box dating to the late 1700's is constructed with tiny square nails and retains its original attic surface. Carolyn tied twigs together to make the primitive window treatment.

The hanging black cupboard over the commode came from a shop in central Ohio and holds an early rye basket.

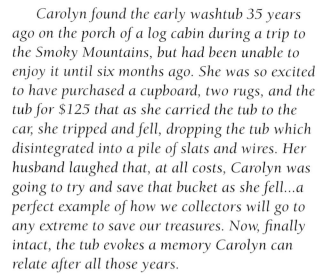

Carolyn found the early washtub 35 years ago on the porch of a log cabin during a trip to the Smoky Mountains, but had been unable to enjoy it until six months ago. She was so excited to have purchased a cupboard, two rugs, and the tub for $125 that as she carried the tub to the car, she tripped and fell, dropping the tub which disintegrated into a pile of slats and wires. Her husband laughed that, at all costs, Carolyn was going to try and save that bucket as she fell...a perfect example of how we collectors will go to any extreme to save our treasures. Now, finally intact, the tub evokes a memory Carolyn can relate after all those years.

When not antiquing, Carolyn works on a project for the City of Ironton to place historical panels downtown to recognize those individuals who influenced the settling and forming of Ironton. Carolyn is also a member and past president of the Ironton Garden Club and the past vice-president of the Lawrence County Historical Society.

Chapter 8

Vera and Fran McCarthy

When I met Vera for the first time, I felt an immediate bond with her. I didn't realize that Vera was ill, as her energy and enthusiasm toward her family and home never indicated that she wasn't well. Since that day, Vera has passed away. I am proceeding to include Fran and Vera's home with her family's permission and encouragement as a testament to Vera's talents. Vera held her mother responsible for her obsession with antiques and "the hunt". When Vera was seven, her mother, an elementary school teacher, took Vera on a field trip to Governor Schuyler's mansion in Albany, New York. From that point Vera was hooked. In fact, she became so interested in antiques that when she learned about Colonial Williamsburg from her fourth grade geography book, Vera went home and ripped up part of the kitchen floor to see if the linoleum concealed wood like that in Williamsburg. Upon arriving home, her mother praised rather than scolded her for being creative! After Vera and Fran were married, Vera continued to utilize her creative talents in decorating their home with a unique combination of old and new, light and dark, and original folk art pieces and heirlooms passed down from her family. Vera also wrote a column called "Observation Point" for the local Lunenburg, Massachusetts newspaper. Fran, who owns a company that produces business forms, is extremely talented in his own right. Fran's talent as an artist and craftsman is displayed throughout the house.

Neighbors and passersby refer to Fran and Vera's home as "the hidden house" because of its concealment among trees and shrubs. They bought the 1899 home in 1970 and added the back wing in the mid-1980's.

A visitor walks through a shaded garden area and patio to enter the house from the side. The olive jar garden ornament is actually a fountain with a quiet bubbler.

Vera placed the basin on top to protect the fountain in the winter and provide a perch for a variety of birds.

Vera waited 30 years for the kitchen of her dreams, and didn't mind waiting three months more for her custom Vermont soapstone counters and sink. She was thrilled with her decision and used mineral oil on it every three months to protect it and create the rich dark patina.

Local craftsman Jeff Dana of Hardwick, Massachusetts, custom designed and built the cupboards. The cupboard above holds some of Vera's Roseville spongeware collection. Fran painted the scene on the plate leaning against the wall.

Vera's wide windowsill over the sink allows extra space to display her shorebirds. The blue vase is a Bank piece, a gift from a friend.

The green cupboard holds more Ohio Roseville spongeware.

The two-handled jug on top is Pennsylvania origin, purchased for its colorful design.

Vera wasn't sure what the multi-drawer cabinet was used for but knew it would be ideal for kitchen storage. Notice the old door used to encase the refrigerator.

The resident cat (it's not real but sure looks it!) naps in an early tote found in a Cape Cod antique shop.

Fran and a local craftsman made the long farm table from 300 year-old boards from an old barn in New Hampshire. The table is pegged and easily seats twelve. The top patina was achieved with tung oil. An early decoy nests in a trencher at the center of the table.

Vera was told by the shop owner that the two-tiered bucket bench with old red paint was from a general store display. Vera used the space to display her cutting boards and other treenware. Fran restored the early cupboard in red above the bench.

The 19thC jelly cupboard in early red wash remains in "as found" condition. It fits perfectly tucked in the corner beneath a 19thC ogee wall clock. The spoon rack, found in a Connecticut antique shop, holds a collection of spoons representing the 13 original colonies. A large unmarked redware bowl sits on top of the cupboard beside a bird's nest containing eggs. The crow on the windowsill is a 1970's crafted piece.

Vera draped pieces of linen through grape vine candle rings suspended from a teacup hook on the inside of the window casing. The treatment allows for texture but at the same time exposes both the molding and the sunlight.

The mustard dry sink came from a local shop and was a "must have". The mirror is a family heirloom and a gift from Fran's mother many years ago.

The built-in cupboard was painted white when Fran and Vera moved into the house. Vera spent one winter and dry scraped the cupboard with a butter knife! It now displays a collection of porcelain, including a large spatterware bowl purchased in Pennsylvania, on the top shelf. The mirrored sconce is a reproduction purchased at a local shop.

The red corner cupboard is new and holds treenware and a peaseware piece.

The cup on the second shelf right was crafted by a now deceased artisan named Aime Lafosse; it is fashioned from spalted birch. The artist wrapped a piece of birch in a towel to dry for years. Only then did the retired insurance broker turned artisan carve the cup.

Vera waited for a long time to purchase the magnificent chest of drawers above in blue paint seen right. It appears to have been a printer's desk as the drawers are divided. The pastoral painting was an anniversary gift to Fran and Vera from their children.

The sitting area reminded Vera of a room in her grandmother's home that she used as a day room. The crewel chairs are crafted with actual crewel fabric from the 1940's. A coverlet is draped over the back of the couch. An early six-board chest serves as a coffee table for the grouping.

A chest resting against the staircase holds a candle and crafted folk art house.

Vera used an old board which she painted mustard and attached an early piece of hardware to hide a thermostat. The wall box also hides a large thermostat.

Fran and Vera purchased the old grain painted table base, circa 1770's, and Fran added the old cutting board top. The child's pinball game with early clay marbles on the table is old. The chair pad seen in the chair on the left is from Family Heirloom Weavers of Pennsylvania.

Fran painted the picture over the mantel, while the whale was carved by Russ Coburn. The iron candleholder is a new piece.

A glass addition off the back of the house overlooks gardens and provides an ideal, bright sitting area on one side and a cozy television area on the other.

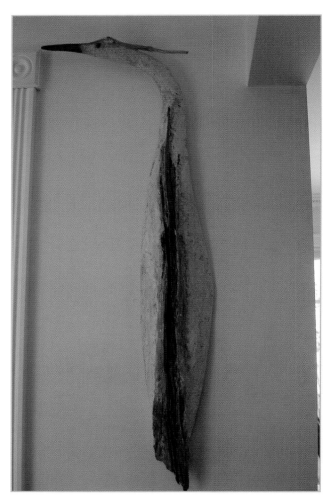

The black plaid chair in the corner was purchased at Homestead Primitives in Fitchburg, Massachusetts.. A small hooked rug protects the top of the chest, seen above

Folk artist Sybille Leary created the white heron hanging beside the doorway. Ms. Leary, originally from Ontario, maintains a studio in Fitzwilliam, New Hampshire, and participates in local shows.

Vera used a patriotic theme in the bathroom. Notice how she used a plastic shower liner along with the tabbed fabric curtain.

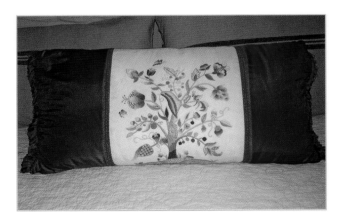

In the 1970's, Fran took his first job as a printer working with a 90 year-old man, who gave him the large roll top desk. It was in pieces but Fran was able to reassemble it and the desk now holds special meaning for him.

The master bedroom trim is painted in Olde Century "Cobblestone" and the bedspread is a Family Heirloom Weavers piece. Fran created the paneling using two old wide picture frames with inserted panels. The pillow shams are Family Heirloom Weavers, as well. The pillow was made using an authentic square of crewel work done by Elsa Williams.

The chest seen left retains its original hardware and wonderful patina; it was a gift to Vera for her birthday. Fran painted the small blue chest now used as a night stand. Roger Boisvert of Homestead Primitives made the blanket crane holding a flag remnant over the mantel. Fran painted the portrait over the mantel, which holds a collection of family photographs.

Roger Boisvert also made the box, shown left, which conceals an air conditioning unit.

Vera used a small balcony off the master bedroom to display a few birdhouses from her collection.

A collection of vintage Christening dresses, one of which was worn by both Vera and her daughters, is displayed over the spool bed in the guestroom.

A grouping of early dolls sits in the small cupboard in the corner of the guestroom.

In the hallway, a mirrored sideboard holds a pair of shoes made for Vera by her shoemaker father when she was 10. She discovered them after her father's death and left them intact with the shoe lasts.

Vera loved signage and used a side of the garage to display some of her favorites. An old grain bin holds a few clay pots.

Vera chose to use the portable fencing, originally used by farmers to direct livestock, as a fence for her small garden. A welcoming pineapple sits beside the gate.

Vera felt that a home should be an extension of oneself and a safe haven and sanctuary. Her home certainly reflects that sentiment and provides a warm and inviting atmosphere for Fran and Vera's three children and six grandchildren.

Chapter 9

❧ ✿ ❧

Judy and Jeff Condon

Although my husband Jeff originally hails from the Buffalo, New York area, Connecticut had been his home for 24 years prior to our move to Virginia in 2002. We were both anxious to return to New England.

We decided to purchase the Massachusetts home described in the Introduction and get a head start on interior work while we still had the luxury of a place to live in Virginia. I had studied the interior of our cape online for almost two years and knew what I wanted to do with regard to major remodeling. A local builder assured us the renovations were structurally possible. We learned that the previous owner, a historian and collector of fine antiques, had passed away in his 90's and that the house was vacant.

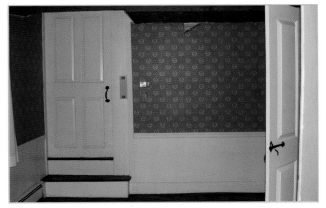

With no immediate plans to occupy the house, we began to tear out walls the day after the closing in early October, 2010. The house featured a small entranceway and a door to the left leading to the kitchen containing a fireplace, center table, and kitchen work area against one wall.

From the kitchen, the wall separated two doors which opened into the small dining area with red print wallpaper.

The kitchen, below, as it appeared prior to purchase of the house.

One of the appealing features, to my thinking, of our 1825 center chimney cape is the steps toward the back that lead in different directions. From the steps, a visitor can head to the old dining room (now kitchen), upstairs, to our 'sunken' bathroom, or to our den that the previous owner used as his bedroom. A small mud room was located at the end of the kitchen counter leading out the back door.

The large fireplace stands on the opposite wall from where the kitchen cabinets were. The front door entranceway can be seen to the right of the fireplace.

The day after the closing I began to strip the wallpaper in all the rooms, which came off much easier than I had anticipated.

Within 24 hours the former dining room looked like the picture seen left. The next day the wall was removed between the former kitchen and dining room. The mudroom walls were also removed and a single post remained to support the beams front to rear.

Then we received an email from our Virginia buyers! They had sold their house and needed ours in four weeks! I commuted between Virginia and Massachusetts, packing or painting depending on where I was resting my head that night. Jeff continued to work in Virginia and pack up the house.

Kitty and I lived in our small RV parked in the driveway in Massachusetts while Jeff came up on weekends. I walked to "work" across the yard each morning to paint followed closely by Kitty-who endeared herself to the workers. Tim, one of the electricians, referred to her as "Boss" when she followed him around the house as he updated the electrical system to accommodate a new heating system.

The ceiling in the former dining area had been taken down after a pipe burst upstairs while the house was vacant. I liked the exposed beams and decided to rip out the rest of the ceiling in what was the former kitchen area to expose those beams as well. For two consecutive weekends in mid-October, the temperature reached the mid to high 70's-so my son, Rich, his friend Jim, Frank, a professional painter, and Frank's nephew camped out on mattresses while they painted the garage, barn, and house. The picture below shows the extent of what I could provide in the way of hearthside cooking!

A header was added to the expanded room with support beams at either end. Unfortunately, since one of the beams needed to be located in the back doorway, the door had to be moved.

We vacated the Virginia property on the agreed upon date and stored our furnishings from a 3700 square foot house in our Massachusetts barn and garage. By then it was mid-November and too cold to remain in the RV, as the storage tanks were at risk of freezing. The house had no heat or water, and Kitty had long since abandoned me for the comfort of the attic eaves despite the lack of heat. I went away for Thanksgiving and returned home to find I had one shower, two toilets, kitchen cabinets, and counters. The floors were still thick with white plaster dust, which I cleaned up repeatedly for weeks. We moved in officially two months after the first swing of the sledge hammer with some details still to be completed-but for the most part our new home was habitable.

The Keeping Room, seen left, was taken from the steps at the end of the former dining room. The 19thC dining room table with original paint and scrub top found in Kentucky was on the cover of my first book, Country on a Shoestring. The blue island is the bottom of a large stepback purchased from Diane Windle in Coatesville, Pennsylvania. The floor cloth under the table was painted by Michelle Hollick of New Hampshire. A stack of bail handled pantry boxes in dry blue paint stands on a blue firkin purchased from coasterpatrick on ebay.

The Ohio cheese safe that I dry scraped down to robin's egg blue holds our everyday yellowware style dishes purchased at Pier 1.

The picture top left shows the wall where the former kitchen counters and cabinets were located. The red dry sink was purchased at The Bowl Barn in Douglas, Massachusetts. The tall red jelly cupboard found in Maine was also on the cover of my first book. It had thick white porch paint that bubbled when I used a heat gun; I dry scraped the cupboard down to its original red wash. The hanging mustard bucket bench over the dry sink was a Pennsylvania find. The tobacco panel window treatments are from Family Heirloom Weavers. An early flax winder make-do stands on the floor beneath the window, a gift to me from my husband.

A small box found at Brimfield holds German stick-legged sheep.

The red standing piece is an early lidded washtub. The black wax pineapple is from Marsh Homestead Country Antiques. The watercolor portraits were done by folk artist Ellen Robertson.

As I've repeatedly said, each of our pieces usually has a memory attached. The hanging carrier is the first small primitive I ever purchased. It was found at a Pennsylvania flea market during the trip to take my eldest daughter to college for her freshman year.

The black whaler's lantern is from Katie's Lighthouse. A dry painted peg rack with mustard paint hangs over the mantel and holds a berry wreath. A built-in chimney cupboard is concealed behind the door to the right of the fireplace.

The hummingbird, my mother's favorite bird, was made by artist Sybille Leary. A small oil on canvas by Christopher Gurshin is displayed in the center of the mantel.

Kitchen cabinets have replaced piles of rubble. A craftsman in New Hampshire made the cabinets, which are primarily drawers that provide easier access to stored items. They are maple rather than pine, as maple tends to expand less when painted. The trim paint in the Keeping Room is Olde Century "Country Red" simulated milk paint. The blue painted bucket bench is from Diane Windle in Pennsylvania. A Shaker working churn in early red wash featuring large hand-carved dovetailed corners stands on the top shelf.

I deliberately left the top walls open to place early cupboards and display painted pieces. The 'Supper Here Today 5-7', most likely an old church sign, was found in Maine.

The small blue hanging cupboard left of the stove is from The Bowl Barn. Early tin shorebirds, many purchased on ebay, stand beside one of folk artist Sybille Leary's woodcocks. The countertops are matt black Formica and the large sink is a Lowe's Franke composite granite piece. The hanging tin cone lights are from Katie's Lighthouse.

I pulled apart a broken wooden box in old dry robin's egg paint purchased from a dealer friend and built the blue cupboard hanging over the dishwasher using old boards I found in the cellar for the back and sides.

Before we leave the Keeping Room, I wanted to show the contrast of my walls before and after I aged them; and it DID make a difference. Pictured below is the wall prior to the aging process.

I used Ralph Lauren Antique Glaze found at Home Depot and had it tinted a color called "Tobacco". Using a good brush, I applied the stain and then 'pulled it out' to the sides, almost drying

the brush as I did so. If too much paint is applied in one spot, it can be removed with a damp cloth. It's easy to apply and fast. I completed the kitchen before I had finished my second cup of tea!

The red hanging cupboard is one I made with a door from the former cupboards. I wanted a small cupboard to fit the narrow space to hold spices; when my search turned up empty, I decided to make my own. The surface is Caromal Colours "Paprika" with their toner applied to the surface.

Before and after views of the hallway are seen below. I removed the black and white toile wallpaper and painted the trim with Olde Century "Linen White".

The former bathroom on the first floor looked brand new. It is a large room measuring approximately 10' X 10' and is located two steps below the hallway. It contained a vanity, tub, built-in ceramic shower, and toilet. While there was nothing wrong with the bathroom, I needed space for a washer and dryer and wanted a larger freestanding shower.

I replaced the ceramic tile with horizontal pine boards. Using a saber saw and a borrowed air gun and compressor, I placed a 10" board on the bottom, then a 12", and another 10" on top. The trim paint is a Benjamin Moore California historical color called "Winter Meadow". The pineapple sconces over the dry sink found in Pennsylvania were made by Katie's Lighthouse. The hammered copper vessel sink is from Lowe's, as is the dark pump. I painted the floor cloth using "Winter Meadow" and flat black paint.

An early tin goose stands on top of a 19thC chest with early black paint. I upended it and use it to store linens.

The hanging pine cupboard over the commode was purchased many years ago from a Vermont dealer at the Farmington Antique Show in Connecticut. An early tin goose is perched on top and the early paint tones blend well with the "Winter Meadow' trim and black.

A signed oil on canvas by the late Mary Beth Baxter hangs to the right of the cupboard.

What was formerly the shower is now an enclosed closet which holds a stacked washer and dryer. When we purchased the house each doorway featured an old paneled door; we removed some to afford more room. One door is repurposed to enclose the washer and dryer.

An oil on board found at a local antique shop depicts a winter scene similar to a favorite Maine vacation spot long visited each year by my family.

Entering through the front door a visitor immediately faces a closet which conceals the center chimney. I used an Olde Century paint called "Old Linen" in all the hallways which provides a neutral color that blends beautifully with every country color. An early blue tin bail handled bucket holds greenery and small silk blue lavender flowers.

Once I had aged the Keeping Room walls, I knew that the front entrance had to be aged as well. A small theorem on velvet done by the late Ann Rea hangs in the corner of the entrance. The wall box is one I painted and lifts to expose a light switch.

The previous owner owned magnificent antiques, many of which were sold at auction in Boston; a few pieces were left behind. The staged stark look of the living room from the front door hallway can be seen left. Jane and Barron Hansen, whose home appeared in "Holidays at a Country Home" in 2011, spent two days with me stenciling the living room.

I removed the door into the back room to gain space. The fireside chair with high sides, one of two,

was purchased at Angel House in Brookfield, Massachusetts, as was the Sheraton couch and scrub top table with red wash base. I tried three different antique area rugs in this room and nothing pulled the gold, red, and blues together. I made the floor cloth on the back of a piece of linoleum purchased at Home Depot for $22.47.

Judy and Jeff Condon 129

The portrait over the small blue jelly cupboard was found in New Hampshire years ago. I actually sold it to a favorite customer in Wisconsin, and then four years later emailed and asked if I could buy it back . . . which I did. The salmon paint-decorated lidded box was an ebay® find.

I found the drop leaf table with breadboard ends in the basement – painted white, rusty and dirty. I cleaned it up and used Caromal Colours Country Living "Paprika" paint to create an aged red look.

A graduated stack of early lidded painted boxes is displayed on top of the two piece 19thC stepback found in Maine. A large handled dry blue painted bucket is filled with bittersweet and sits on top. On the far left is a mallard shaped pewter candlestick made by my mother. The iron candlestick was made by blacksmith Kathy Nugent as a gift.

Three 19thC watercolors hang behind the bittern. The top portrait is unsigned. The middle portrait depicts Robert Hopkins by Justus Dalee, while the bottom picture is a signed William Mercle and dated 1820.

I purchased the two-door cupboard with red wash to hang over the stove in the kitchen but it proved a bit too large. A tin shorebird rests on an architectural piece. The Windsor chair is new. The hanging candleholder was made by Kathy Nugent, a renowned blacksmith from Kansas who sells her pieces through her company, Primitives. The theorem on canvas was made by Jane Hansen.

Two reproduction Windsor chairs provide additional seating when needed. The spoon rack on the wall was fashioned by Nelson Ruffin of New Hampshire.

The picture left shows a built-in cupboard (formerly open) and entrance to a small hallway that leads to the Keeping Room on the other side.

Using one of the original doors from the house, we enclosed the open cupboard which now holds movies and books. In the short hallway are two small pantries and the basement entrance. The theorem on velvet to the right of the cupboard depicts a Shaker village done by the late Ann Rea.

Judy and Jeff Condon 131

Early leather bound books, German wooly sheep, and a 19thC German Noah's Ark decorate the mantel. The theorem on canvas was done by Jane Hansen.

The room at the rear of the house is part of a small addition added in 1899, indicated by the dated newspapers we found in the wall. This room was used by the previous owner as his bedroom; we now use it as our sitting room and my office. Working conditions were stressful for a few weeks as the ceiling was ripped out to provide a 'chase' to the second floor where a second bathroom was being added. We exposed the vertical beam and another in the ceiling. The blue chest was a find at a flea market in Connecticut. The trim paint is Olde Century Olde Ivory. The 'Apples For Sale' sign was purchased at the Farmington, Connecticut Antique Show and features dry country red, blue, and mustard original paint.

The long neck paper mache and driftwood heron is another creation by artist Sybille Leary.

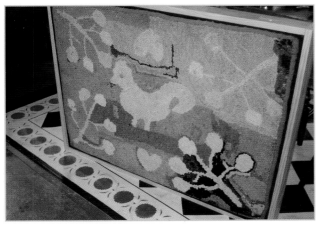

The early hooked rug was found in New Hampshire last summer. I love the lollipop flowers in each corner and the one small section of blue wool that blends beautifully with the early blue painted pieces in the room. The naïve animal seems to be a 'composite' but I believe it is more rooster than any other.

This is our TV room but I didn't want the flat screen to be an eyesore. I made a wooden frame for the rug using 1" X 3" boards and painted the frame flat black; it conceals the TV perfectly.

The early box with paint conceals the DVD player and cable box.

The blue cupboard is the top of the blue base that I use as an island in the Keeping Room.

The Boardman Wells clock shown above right dates to the early 19thC and was a gift from my mother-in-law. It features wooden gears and a 12-hour mechanism. The painting on the glass front is the same pattern embossed on the pendulum.

The blue stepback was found in Maine but is a Virginia Shenandoah Valley piece; it was sold to the dealer in Maine so the Virginian could pay his taxes. I found the canvas goose on top at an antique shop in South Carolina.

The shelves hold a collection of early German buildings, sheep, and Noah's Arks. Small birds are seen on the bottom shelf in front of early pewter plates.

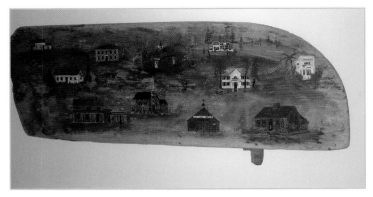

After I found an early wheelbarrow side with original dry paint, I commissioned Barron Hansen (see Holidays at a Country Home) to paint what I call "the story of us". It depicts the homes Jeff and I lived in as children, a schoolhouse to represent my career and a wagon to represent his with the bearing industry, homes where we have lived and even Kitty sitting next to the Virginia house. The panel hangs over my desk.

A 19thC robin's egg blue cupboard holds a collection of early dry painted buckets. The lift top blanket chest below dates to the early 1700's and features a single 30" board front and back and original snipe hinges. The board in the back is affixed with large hand-forged rosehead nails.

The trencher with superb original blue paint is filled with Bellini apples; it was found at the Seville Antique Center in Ohio. The 19thC watercolor portrait of a sea captain was purchased from Bobbie Preiss Antiques in Ohio; I couldn't resist the sitter's blue coat. The mallard duck is a driftwood and paper mache creation by Sybille Leary; its beak is a large nail.

Seen above, the view from the kitchen area looks through the back hallway to the den. The stairs to the second floor are on the right. About the stairs! They don't look very steep but I have to "hike" up them. I was sitting at my desk working when one of the young men installing ducts trudged up. I listened as he thumped (pause), thumped (pause) . . . I yelled to him, "You sound like how I feel when I go up those stairs." He replied, "Yeah, these are really steep and it's harder if you're tall". I replied, "Yeah? What about old?" Even Kitty sits at the bottom with a look of disdain before taking a running leap!

Three early painted gameboards are displayed on the side wall. On top of the stairs, my favorite gameboard is an old chipped red and black board on heavy sheet metal.

The master bedroom has a ceiling that is only 6' high. A small single closet was inadequate for us.

A library off the master bedroom was ideal for adding a second full bathroom and a large walk-in closet.

The shelves in the library were wonderful and I wanted to retain as many as space would permit. The shelves along the right, seen left, were removed to accommodate the closet, a second sink, a vanity, and commode. I wanted to preserve the window, which left spaces that were dimensionally non-standard. Rather than spend thousands of dollars for custom-made vanities, I found two identical kitchen cabinet bases in stock for $387 at Home Depot, and two pine-laminated boards for $25 at Lowe's.

The old buggy bench was 1" too wide to fit under the window because of the iron back and side rails, so I removed the iron piece and stored it; the bench fits perfectly.

I used Minwax "Early American" stain and had our carpenter cut and insert the oval sink to create the top. Because the pipes had to enter from the side, an 8" gap was created between the wall and the vanity. I built a panel for each vanity which resembles a door and allows access to the plumbing; esthetically, I think the panel improved the overall appearance.

The walk-in closet is located on the right. The shelves provide a gallery for family photos.

Our bed is high and I use bed steps. The space between the high bed and low ceiling is quite cozy, although it creates an illusion of being 10 feet off the floor. The duvet in navy and cream linen is from Family Heirloom Weavers. I used "Prushian Blue" paint from The Seraph on the trim in the bedroom and "Linen White" in the bathroom. I used Family Heirloom Weaver's *tobacco linen panels* for the window treatments.

The Family Heirloom Weaver coverlet hanging on the blanket crane conceals a flat screen television. The six-board chest below dates to the mid 18thC and retains the original snipe hinges and lift-top insert. A large primitive doll sits atop the cable box.

A stack of fabric covered pantry boxes holds some of my costume jewelry. The hooked rug showing our first cat, Kitty1, and Kitty2, our present cat whom you met in my book The Warmth of Home, was hooked by Lisa Baughman of Pennsylvania.

The guestroom is two steps down from the landing at the top of the stairs.

We removed the carpeting on the stairs, then sanded and stained them. The guestroom is painted with Olde Century Barn Red paint. The brick red and tan coverlet is from Family Heirloom Weavers.

I purchased the 'Tree of Life' hooked rug on ebay, as the colors blend beautifully with the room's tan and brick tones.

In the spring, I look forward to planting my gardens and creating a quiet retreat around the flagpole. Blessed with a wealth of raspberry bushes, I look forward to once more making jam, something I've been unable to do since we left Connecticut nine years ago.

Prior to owning the house, I told a friend that I envisioned myself going out a screen door at the back of the house to the stone patio and meadow. She asked, "Do you hear the door slam?" – to which I responded, "Yes!" Unable to find a contractor to build the door when hot weather suddenly arrived, I built my own to resemble an early wooden door using repurposed corner metal braces and early hinges taken from interior doors.

We were fortunate to find a home so lovingly cared for by the previous owner. His meticulous attention to the house and surrounding meadows and woods allowed us to focus mostly on "wants" rather than "needs".

In the barn, we have set up six beds on the second floor and made it into a bunk house for grandchildren. Jeff plans to convert the first floor into a "man cave". Who knows – maybe you'll see the before and after of that project in the future.

Some of you might recall that I like to paint a roof and have had great success doing so with Behr roof paint. We had the roof on the barn and garage power washed and then had them painted a flat black to match the roof on the house.

During the summer, our godchild, Randy, from St Maarten came for a two week visit and while here painted all the outdoor white wicker furniture a mocha brown. It greatly improved the appearance on the patio and blended much more effectively with the color of the house.

Despite a cold winter with heavy snowfall, our return to New England and a home that closely resembles the 1764 farmhouse we purchased when Jeff and I first married has changed the course of our lives. Being close to family, to travel down New England country roads within minutes of antique shops, to surround myself with 19thC architecture, to pass village greens with white churches and steeples, has made me realize how good it is to be Back Home again.

The renovations I dreamed of and planned for over two years, finally realized, were worth the work and stress . . . I think! Would I do it again? I don't think so, although Jeff, who knows me better than perhaps I know myself, isn't at all convinced.

The "simply country" book series

by Judy Condon

Country on a Shoestring
- 33 tips on how to decorate on a shoestring

Of Hearth and Home
- mantels, old painted pieces, signs and primitives

A Simpler Time
- log homes, bedrooms, kitchens, dining rooms, folk art and stencils

Country Decorating for All Seasons
- holiday doors, porches, mantels, trees, vignettes; summer gardens, and fall decorating

As Time Goes By
- The Keeping Room; boxes, baskets and bowls; The Privy; Hallways and Small Ways; The Guest Room

Country at Heart
- The Tavern Room; early looms, dolls and bears; The Gathering Room; a kitchen aged to perfection; country gardens

Welcome Home
- Over 350 photographs from 2 Connecticut homes and 5 Ohio homes.

Home Again
- A house tour book featuring 1 Maine home and 7 Ohio homes including a never before photographed Shaker collection.

The Warmth of Home
- 3 Massachusetts homes, 1 Pennsylvania home, 3 Ohio homes, 1 New York home and 1 Delaware home

The Country Home
- 6 Ohio homes, 2 Massachusetts homes, and 1 New Hampshire home

The "simply country" book series
(continued)

The Comfort of Home
- Over 325 color photographs showing a Massachusetts and Ohio home of two exceptional collectors. A Maine home; three Massachusetts homes, one of which is in the city.

Simple Greens – Simply Country
- Over 400 color photographs of country homes decorated for the holidays. Also a chapter on "how to make a country bed" and the recipe for the large decorative gingerbread boys and pantry cakes.

The Country Life
- The home of antique dealer, Marjorie Staufer of Ohio and Colette Donovan of Massachusetts is featured, as well as 4 other Massachusetts homes, a Maine home, a New Hampshire home and a Connecticut home of children's book author, Mark Kimball Moulton.

Simply Country Gardens
- Over 500 color photographs of "just country gardens" from twenty-three homes.

The Spirit of Country
- A house tour format book featuring homes in Virginia, Maine, Connecticut, Indiana, Ohio, Massachusetts, New Hampshire and Kentucky.

The Joy of Country
- Over 400 pictures of homes in Wisconsin, Upstate New York, Ohio, a Connecticut 18thC home, a doublewide in Delaware, 5 Massachusetts homes, a Pennsylvania home and a Maryland home converted from a 19thC granary.

Holidays at a Country Home
- The third holiday book in the series consists of over 500 color photographs of 13 decorated homes and a Condon traditional secret recipe!

A Touch of Country
- *A Touch of Country* features 8 homes. A unique collection of stoneware and weathervanes is included in one home; primitive settings and collections of early paint are highlights. Rug hookers will love one of the chapters and the avid antique collector will marvel over a Maine home!